Paper Route

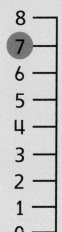

Written by Jack Manson

Photographs by John Paul Endress

Celebration Press

Parsippany, New Jersey

8
7
6
5
4
3
2
1
0

8
7
6
5
4
3
2
1
0

3

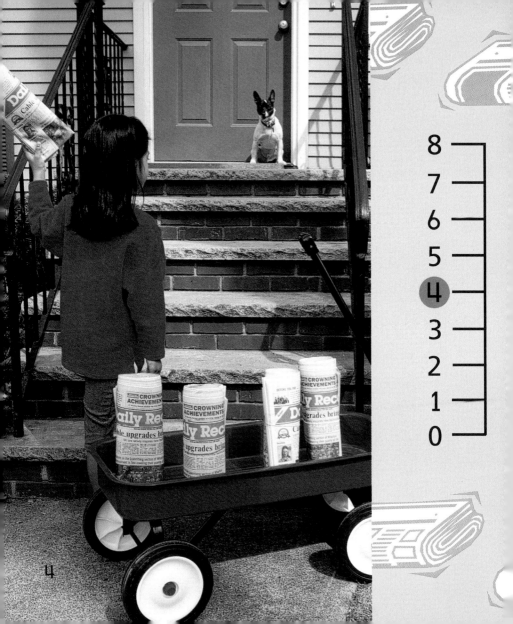

8
7
6
5
4
3
2
1
0

4

US MAIL

8
7
6
5
4
3
2
1
0

6

8
7
6
5
4
3
2
1
0

8

God and You

The ABC's of Faith

Written by Francine M. O'Connor

Illustrated by Kathryn Boswell

Catechetical Advisors:
Redemptorist Fathers

LIGUORI
PUBLICATIONS

One Liguori Drive
Liguori, Missouri 63057
(314) 464-2500

Imprimi Potest
Edmund T. Langton, C.SS.R.
Provincial, St. Louis Province
The Redemptorists

Imprimatur:
+John N. Wurm, S.T.D., Ph.D.
Vicar General, Archdiocese of St. Louis

Cover Design: Jim Corbett

Table of Contents

Introduction

One thing I have learned after years of working with children is that God cannot be "taught." From the moment of birth, God is already a very real part of every child's world. All we adults can hope to do is to help children to recognize him in all that they experience. To do this we have to back up and remember how the world looks from the eyes of a child. Francis Thompson's poem *Shelley* says it well:

> Know you what it is to be a child?
> It is to be something very different
>   from the man of today.
> It is to have a spirit yet streaming
>   from the waters of baptism;
> it is to believe in love,
>   to believe in loveliness,
> to believe in belief.
>
> It is to be so little
>   that the elves can reach
>   to whisper in your ear;
> it is to turn pumpkins into coaches,
>   and mice into horses,
> lowness into loftiness,
>   and nothing into everything,
> for each child has its fairy godmother
>   in its soul.

May these pages penetrate into that magic world where God mingles with elves and fairy godmothers and becomes the ultimate reality.

F.M.O.

That
Super Spectacular
Someone – You!

Not too many years ago,
God the Father, the People-Maker,
looked at Mommy and Daddy and said,
"Your love is just the right kind of love
to make a super spectacular someone."
And he made YOU!

And he made you oh so very little,
so that you could fit into Mommy's arms
and be right up close to Daddy's smile,
and you learned their special kind of loving.

And he gave you the beautiful gift of life,
and he let Mommy and Daddy give you everything else,
like food and clothes and toys and games,
and you learned their special way of giving.

And he made you just a helpless babe,
so that they could teach you right from the start
how to walk and how to talk and
how to love the things God made,
and you learned their special style of loving!
    AND LOOK AT YOU TODAY!

Tall as Daddy's belt buckle — almost!
Surprising as the Fourth of July,
with a smile that makes me want
to smile back.

Learning new things every day,
like making your bed and writing your name
and making people laugh with your silly stories.

Always ready to be a big help,
always knowing when Mommy needs a hug
or Daddy wants a lap-sitter to cuddle for a while.

Now! Wasn't that clever of God to do that,
to make you just the way that you are,
to create you out of your parents' love
and let them help you to learn and grow
and become the super spectacular someone
that he had planned you to be not too long ago?

7

God Loves You — Count the Ways

God is LOVE —
that's what St. John tells us
and St. John ought to know
for he walked right beside Jesus
many, many years ago.

And LOVE is what God and Jesus
are really all about,
selfishness upside down
and anger turned inside out.

See if you can count how many times
Jesus told us to LOVE.

First he said "LOVE God with all your heart,"
and "LOVE your neighbor" is the other part.
He said "LOVE one another" and that's not hard to do,
but remember he said "LOVE your enemy too."

He said "The ones who LOVE me will keep my word
and heaven will be their special reward."
For "the Father will know that you are my friends
by the way that you LOVE me and keep my commands."

He also said "The greatest LOVE in this land
is the man who will give up his life for a friend."
And that's just what *he* did for you and for me
and we learned how *really* hard LOVE can be.

St. John was right, wouldn't you say?
God is LOVE in every way.

Whenever you are thinking about God,

G
think about LOVE!
D

And when you are thinking about Love,

L
think about GOD!
V
E

What Elton the Elephant Almost Forgot

Elton the Elephant was an unhappy beast
from deep in the jungle, so far away.
He would look at himself in the Great Mirror Lake
and ask the same questions day after day.

"Why am I ugly and clumsy and fat,
and why such a dull color gray?
I have no soft mane like handsome King Lion,
no bright flashy feathers like the parrots gay,
no long tail for swinging like my monkey friends,
just why did God make me this way?"

His Mom would say, "Elton, do not question God.
He made you the way that he wants you to be."
But Elton kept grumbling till that terrible day
When King Lion was trapped 'neath a fallen tree.

10

The parrots were squawking and flying about,
the monkeys were skittering to and fro,
King Lion was roaring in pain and in fear,
till Elton just lifted the tree — nice and slow.

The whole jungle cheered and they had a great feast,
and they carved Elton's name in the trunk of that tree.
Elton's mother smiled proudly and said to her son,
"What a nice, helpful creature God made you to be."

Now Elton the Elephant is the happiest beast,
beloved by his jungle sisters and brothers,
'cause he knows God gave him his own special gifts
to help the Lord Jesus by helping all others.

The Alphabet Way to God

Here are some words to help you to remember God
every time you say your alphabet:

Adore means to love God the very most, and
Beautiful are the things that he made.
Church is our place to visit him, and
Divine means all things holy and good.
Eternity is togetherness with God all the time in a
Forever-place that Christians call heaven.
Goodness is anything touched by God's hand, and
Holy is how we feel when we pray.
I is the special name we have for ourselves, friends of
Jesus, God's Son and our Brother, who is
King of all heaven and angels and men.
Love is all that God asks us to do, and
Mankind are the people we love, and
Now is the time for us to begin by

Offering our love to our friends.
Perfect is what God is and what we try to be, and
Quiet-time is for thinking about that.
Remembering God is a good way to pray, and a
Saint is what praying will make us.
Today is the day that reminds us that he
Understands that every child needs
Violets and bluebirds and tall, shady trees,
Woodlands and green grass and love.
X-cited is how I feel when I think about
You and the way God made you so fine
    and the
Zillion other things he does for us all
    every minute, every hour,
    all the time!

Secrets of the First Christmas

The shepherds knew
on that first Christmas morn,
when angels sang on their quiet hill,
that a Savior had come
to Bethlehem town
to bring peace to men of good will.

BUT THEY DIDN'T KNOW
WHAT WE KNOW!
That the little Child
with the gentle smile
was really God's very own Son,
and he came to tell us
of his Father's love
and how heaven could be won.

The Wise Men knew
a King had been born
when they saw a star from miles away.
They followed its light
all through the night
to find the place where the baby King lay

BUT THEY DIDN'T KNOW WHAT WE KNOW!
That the baby King
so tiny and new
was a King who would rule so grand,
not just for a while
but forever and ever
in people's hearts all over the land.

So it would have been nice
to be in that place
where God's own baby Son was born,
to march right on down
through Bethlehem town
and see him smile on the first Christmas morn.

BUT CHRISTMAS IS EVEN NICER TODAY!
Because *we* know that Jesus
is our brother and friend;
he made lame men walk and blind men see,
he fed the hungry
and helped the poor
and said, "Let the children come unto me."

Climb Up with Jesus

THIS IS A CLIMBING-UP STORY — YOU READ IT FROM BOTTOM TO TOP.
JUST START ON THE FIRST STEP LIKE JESUS DID — AND CLIMB WITH HIM ALL
THE WAY UP.

Mary
to th
and
for tl

In a tiny stable in
the Infant Jesus w
God placed a brig
so the people cou

Mary went with Joseph to Betl
to obey the law of the land,
and, since God had decided th
they were also obeying God's

It all began with a giant love,
God's love for his people on earth,
and through our loving Mother, Mary,
he arranged for his Son's special birth.

16

Jesus has gone to heaven now
to rule over all of the land,
and yet he is only a prayer away
when we need a helping hand.

Jesus loved us all so much
he suffered and died for our sins,
to show us the way to heaven
and to teach us the way we should love.

When Jesus was twelve, he got lost.
His folks searched all over for him.
They found him in the Temple in town,
teaching God's Word to the priests.

seph took the Baby
s at a nearby church,
e cried, "Look, the Lord has come,"
w he was God right away.

wn,
1.
up in the sky
his Son.

ago,

A Brand New Year
to Grow In

Here comes January,
   when the moon is silver
   and the air is cold
   and the morning world sparkles
   with last night's frost
   and a New Year begins again —
A brand-new, unused, waiting year,
an after-Christmas gift from God
   to grow a little taller in,
   to learn more about Jesus in,
   to be better than you were last year in —
Three hundred and sixty-five new mornings
   for thanking God for another day,
   for helping Mommy around the house,
   for giving hugs and kisses away —
And fifty-two Sundays to visit Jesus,
   to love him and be near him at Mass,
   to kneel before him when you pray —
Another spring for sailing kites in,
   for planting seeds in,
   for watching trees turn green in —

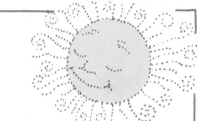

And another Easter full of joy
   because of Jesus never dying,
   because of God being with us always —
And another summer of vacation fun,
   for splashy swimming on sunny days,
   for quiet fishing on cool, clear lakes —
And another brightly painted fall
   for crackly walks on fallen leaves,
   for Halloween trick-or-treating,
   and Thanksgiving turkey eating —

And another Christmas
   for ending the year with loving and giving,
   for saying happy birthday to God's only Son,
   for looking back on another year gone
   and thanking the Father for life.

I have something nice for YOU!
See if you can tell me what it is
It comes with every Valentine,
but it is not RED!

It warms you like big Mister Sun,
but it is not ROUND!

It is soft, like a cuddly kitten
sleeping in your lap;
And fun, like a wiggly puppy
licking at your face.

Sometimes it is very quiet (Shh!)
like a clock that ticks at night.
Sometimes it makes a HAPPY
  noise
like the band in a big parade!

You cannot taste it or smell it,
or hold it in your hand:
But you *always* know who has it . . .
Mother has it in her voice,
when she tucks you in bed at night,
Daddy has it in his arms
when he gives you his BIGGEST hug!

And grandma has it in her smile
every time you visit her.

On Sunday morning
the whole family brings it to God,
because that is where it belongs,
because that is where it *begins*.

Do you know what it is yet?
I will spell it for you . . .
   L - O - V - E !! That's right, it's LOVE.
St. John says that God is Love
— and know what?
   HE REALLY IS!!!!

HAPPY ST. VALENTINE'S DAY, LITTLE FRIENDS

Easter Wonder

One little daisy
Growing in a field
Is pretty!

BUT OH, OH!

A dried-up daisy
Dropping its petals
Is not!

Wait now * * Something wonderful is happening!
Winter comes * * Then spring will follow * * And
look!

Two, four, six, eight, ten new daisies * * Growing
where there once was one!

A furry caterpillar
Crawling on a leaf
Is fun!

BUT OH, OH!

A gray cocoon
Curled on a stick
Is not!

Wait now * * Something wonderful is happening!
A little while * * The cocoon will open * * And look!
A butterfly, black and yellow and purple,
spreads giant wings and flies away!

Stories of Jesus —
His friends and his life
Are wonderful!

BUT OH, OH!

Jesus dead
Upon his Cross
Is not!

Wait now * * Something wonderful is happening!
Jesus alive * * Talking with friends * * Talking with us * * Giving his love!
Jesus alive and as near as our very next prayer * * Jesus alive forever!

Not dying is what this story is all about,
And Easter is God's undying promise to you!

THE BEGINNING

Hey, God, Summer Is Here!

Yesterday I saw a frog
  sunning himself on a lily pad.
He told me, "Summer is here!"

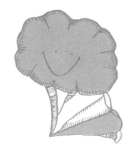

And yesterday I saw a petunia
  open her petals and smile at me.
She told me, "Summer is here!"

And yesterday I saw a yellow bee
  take a sip of a marigold.
He told me, "Summer is here!"

And yesterday I overheard Michael
  talking to God in his prayers.
He said, "Hey, God, summer is here!"

And Michael ran out to find his friends,
and hand in hand
they rolled on the soft, green hillside
and climbed up the big giant trees
and swam in the bubbly, cold river
and sang a thank-you song to God.

For summer is really, truly here
and summer means fun and friendship
and flowers and frogs
and bees and trees
and being a rolling,
climbing,
swimming,
singing part
of this wonderful summer world that God has made!

"Hey, God, that was a neat thing to do!"

If I Were a Mockingbird

If I were a maple tree,
I'd stretch up on my tippytoes
and grow as tall as I could be
and spread my branches way out far
to shade the warm, soft earth below
and I'd thank my God for making me!

If I were a mockingbird,
I'd build a nest for my family
and hide it in the maple tree.
Then I'd fly up to the topmost branch
and sing out with my sweetest song
to thank my God for making me!

If I were a daffodil,
I'd wear my brightest yellow gown
to match the sunlight shining down,
and join my friends upon the hill
bowing in the summer breeze
and thank my God for making me!

If I were a summer breeze,
I'd rustle the leaves of the maple tree
and tickle the baby mockingbirds,
and hug each yellow daffodil
dancing on the sunlit hill,
and thank my God for making me!

But since I am just a little child,
I'll sit beneath the maple tree
and let the warm breeze kiss my cheek
while daffodils dance about my feet.
And I will sing like the mockingbird sings
and thank my God for EVERYTHING!

Finding God on a Summer Day

Here is a beautiful summer day!

I can see so many things that God put there just for me.
I will tell you about a few of them,
and you can find the rest.

The sunshine was put there by God for me
yellow and round and shimmery bright,
drying me off after an afternoon's swim or
getting in my eyes while I'm watching the
birds or
shining on everything in sight or
waking up the flowers and making them
bloom.

28

The tree was put there by God for me,
growing up straight and tall and strong,
a place to climb and look around or
a cool, shady tent to cover me or
a quiet place to sit and read or
a base for playing hide-and-seek.

The lake was put there by God for me,
like a big, blue sky lying down or
a splishy-splashy swimming place or
a mirror for an upside-down world or
a treasure of fish for me to catch
and smooth white rocks to collect.

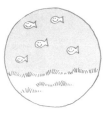

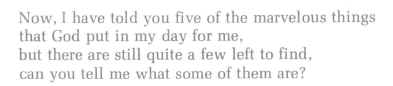

The grass was put there by God for me,
dewy-soft and emerald green,
a plushy carpet for rolling around on or
a sweet-smelling, sitting-down picnic place or
a lying-down place for watching the clouds or
a tall, grassy forest for tiny bugs.

The flowers were put there by God for me,
yellow, red, blue — all of the crayon colors,
a nice bouquet to bring home to mother or
a resting spot for the butterflies or
a honey treat for the bees to sip or
just a beautiful look-at gift for my eyes.

Now, I have told you five of the marvelous things
that God put in my day for me,
but there are still quite a few left to find,
can you tell me what some of them are?

And when you go out into your *own* summer day
See what God put there for YOU!

Thank You, God

hank you, Father, for happy things
like silly days with my best friend,
like riding high on Daddy's strong shoulders,
like bird-songs and breezes and dry, crackly leaves.

nd thank you, Father, for quiet things
like being together at the end of the day,
like the soft, warm bed where happy dreams wait,
like the snowflakes that fall in the middle of the night.

nd thank you, Father, for helpful things
like the bedtime stories that Mommy reads,
like walks in the woods when the leaves turn bright,
like teachers and neighbors and our parish priest.

nd thank you, Father, for loving things
like the spicy-kitchen smell of food on the stove,
like Mommy's arms when everything goes wrong,
like a phone call from someone far away.

ather, you care for all of us,
every day of the year.
Thank you for this special day
to think about your care.

nd help the families all over the world,
especially those who are poor or sad,
to remember how much you love them today,
so they will have the same happiness we've had.

Other ABC's Books

THE ABC'S OF THE MASS . . . for Children
This creative combination of verse and illustration moves step-by-step through the various parts of the Mass and includes simplified versions of many of the prayers that little ones hear every Sunday — but don't really understand. **$2.50**

THE ABC'S OF THE ROSARY . . . for Children
This little book does more than merely teach the formula and the prayers — it highlights each of the fifteen mysteries in a fascinating presentation that brings the story of Jesus to life. This book makes the rosary a prayer experience the whole family can share. **$2.50**

THE ABC'S OF THE SACRAMENTS . . . for Children
This booklet introduces children to both familiar and yet-to-be experienced sacraments. It touches on each of these important elements of faith with verses and illustrations that celebrate God's loving presence at these special moments. **$2.50**

THE ABC's OF THE OLD TESTAMENT . . . for Children
The Old Testament is a mighty big book for little children, but *The ABC's of the Old Testament* makes it just the right size. The book introduces little ones to the Hebrew people and brings the time before Christ to life. Includes the stories of Creation, Noah, Abraham, Ruth, Moses, and many more. **$2.50**

Order from your local bookstore or write to:
Liguori Publications, Box 060, Liguori, Missouri 63057-9999
*(Please add $1.00 for postage and handling for
orders under $5.00; add $1.50 for orders over $5.00.)*